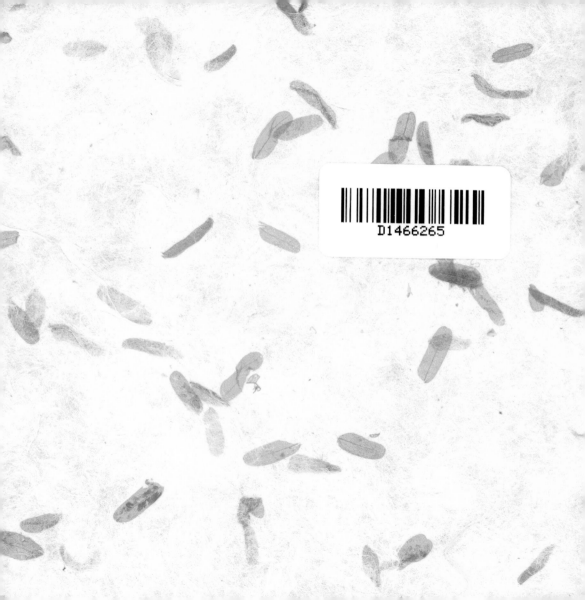

The Language of
BRIDES

*A Blue Mountain Arts® Collection
in Celebration of Brides*

Blue Mountain Press ™

SPS Studios, Inc., Boulder, Colorado

Library of Congress Catalog Card Number: 2001000084
ISBN: 0-88396-586-0

ACKNOWLEDGMENTS appear on page 48.

Certain trademarks are used under license.

Manufactured in Thailand
First Printing: March 2001

 This book is printed on recycled paper.

Library of Congress Cataloging-in-Publication Data

The language of brides : a Blue Mountain Arts collection.
    p.   cm.
  ISBN 0-88396-586-0 (alk. paper)
  1. Marriage—Quotations, maxims, etc. 2. Weddings—Quotations, maxims, etc.
  3. Marriage—Poetry. 4. Weddings—Poetry.
  PN6084.M3 L36 2001
  306.81—dc21

                                                2001000084
                                                  CIP

SPS Studios, Inc.
P.O. Box 4549, Boulder, Colorado 80306

 Contents

(Authors listed in order of first appearance)

To the Bride

May your wishes for a lifetime
   of happiness be granted.
May you and your husband always be
   a source of comfort and support
         for each other —
not only in times of need,
but when things are going well.
May you always be as polite
   to each other
as you would be to a stranger.
May you recognize that neither of you
is responsible for the other's
   pain or happiness.
May you understand that respect is
   the key to a lasting relationship.
May you permit one another to
   continue to expand and develop.

May you always find peace in your home.
May you always be faithful to one another.
May you always stay flexible enough
    to listen and consider each other's opinion.
May you always find ways to strengthen
    your bond with one another.
May you be fully aware that neither of you
    will ever be able to fill all the needs
    of the other.
May you continue to discover
    similar interests.
May you appreciate each other's
    good qualities and always focus
        on the positive.
May your affection for one another
    never cease,
but instead continue to grow —
becoming a deeper, richer,
    and never-ending love.

   Deborah T. Kinnebrew

Love Is What
Marriage Is All About

Love is being happy for the other person
　　when they are happy
　　being sad for the person when they are sad
　　being together in good times
　　and being together in bad times
Love is the source of strength

Love is being honest with yourself at all times
　　being honest with the other person at all times
　　telling, listening, respecting the truth
　　and never pretending
Love is the source of reality

Love is an understanding so complete that
　　you feel as if you are a part of the other person
　　accepting the other person just the way they are
　　and not trying to change them
　　to be something else
Love is the source of unity

Love is the freedom to pursue your own desires
     while sharing your experiences with the other person
     the growth of one individual alongside of
     and together with the growth
     of another individual
Love is the source of success

Love is the excitement of planning things together
     the excitement of doing things together
Love is the source of the future

Love is the fury of the storm
     the calm in the rainbow
Love is the source of passion

Love is giving and taking in a daily situation
     being patient with each other's needs and desires
Love is the source of sharing

Love is knowing that the other person
     will always be with you
     regardless of what happens
     missing the other person when they are away
     but remaining near in heart at all times
Love is the source of security

Love is the source of life

 Susan Polis Schutz

The most wonderful
of all things in life,
I believe, is the discovery
of another human being
with whom one's relationship
has a glowing depth, beauty,
and joy as the years increase.
This inner progressiveness
of love between
two human beings
is a most marvelous thing.
It cannot be found
by looking for it or
by passionately wishing for it.
It is a sort of Divine accident.

 Sir Hugh Walpole

There is only one happiness in life, to love and be loved.

 George Sand

Two souls with but a single thought,
Two hearts that beat as one.

 Friedrich Halm

Within the circle of its love,
marriage encompasses all of life's most important relationships.
A wife and a husband are each other's best friend,
confidant, lover, teacher, listener, and critic....
Marriage deepens and enriches every facet of life.
Happiness is fuller; memories are fresher; commitment is stronger;
even anger is felt more strongly, and passes away more quickly.

 Edmund O'Neill

There is no more lovely, friendly and
charming relationship, communion or
company than a good marriage.

 Martin Luther

A marriage...
makes of two fractional lives a whole;
it gives to two purposeless lives
a work, and doubles the strength
of each to perform it;
it gives to two
questioning natures
a reason for living,
and something to live for;
it will give a new gladness
to the sunshine,
a new fragrance to the flowers,
a new beauty to the earth,
and a new mystery to life.

 Mark Twain

Planning Your Wedding

It's true. You have many decisions to be made with regard to planning your wedding. But you've already made the most important decision of all... that of offering to share your life and your love with another in a truly holy communion.

— Douglas Pagels

We have looked back to the days before our wedding many times. It's often been a source of strength for us to know that we could plan something so important together and have the outcome be a true expression of our love. Because we each made a conscious effort to share the planning tasks as equally as possible, our wedding day and vows meant so much to both of us... and we've never forgotten their importance.

— Emily Chase

The whole process, painful as it was at times, taught us a great deal about solving problems, showing patience, focusing on what was truly important. And looking back, it's clear the wedding became a metaphor for how we would live our lives together.

— Cokie and Steve Roberts

We made a decision early on in the planning of our wedding that no matter what happened, no matter what went wrong or what was less than perfect, no matter who messed up their entrances or their lines, or who was late or didn't show up at all, we were going to laugh about it and enjoy ourselves. And that's exactly what we did. Our day couldn't have been more perfect. It went off without a hitch. This is YOUR day! You have been looking forward to it all your life! Enjoy it! Let nothing hinder it. Have fun with it all and don't worry about details. Think about waking up every day next to the man you love most.

Anonymous

Don't let the planning of your wedding overshadow the ultimate goal — the important thing is that you get to spend the rest of your life with the one you love. And though the process may test your relationship at times, working toward that moment when you get to say "I do" should be a time to strengthen your love.

Jane Andrews

♡ Share This Special Time With... ♡

Sisters

Sitting on my bed,
Sharing sister secrets,
We whispered our dreams
Like wishes on the wind.
Today one wish comes true.
It's a whole new beginning.
A new path I will walk
With my husband,
And with you, my sister.
I will still need you,
For you are my forever friend.
And I will still need time
To sit on my bed,
Share sister secrets,
And whisper dreams
Like wishes on the wind.

♡ Judy Edwards

Brothers

Are there any brothers
who do not criticize a bit and
make fun of the fiancé who is
stealing a sister from them?

♡ Colette

Bridesmaids

A happy bridesmaid makes a happy bride.

♡ ♡ Alfred, Lord Tennyson

Friends

I am who I am
Because of the balance
Friends give my life.
Without friends, my life
And my wedding
Would be incomplete.

♡ Judy Edwards

♡♡ ...And Remember the Love ♡♡ of Your Parents

We look at you now —
so happy and so in love —
excited like a child about the new life
    that lies ahead for you
and the man you have chosen
    to share it with.
Although now you are a
    successful young woman,
you are still and always will be our little girl.
We're so proud of you today
and so happy that you have
    found this special man.
Today, as we watch you walk down the aisle —
the most beautiful girl in the world —
our hearts will just be bursting with pride.
Enjoy today, darling Daughter;
enjoy the life you now have.
Remember that we will always
    be here for you,
and we could never love you more
    than we do on this, your wedding day.

♡ Kym A. Innes

 *The Dress...*

There is something about a wedding-gown prettier than in any other gown in the world.

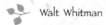 Douglas Jerrold

The white bride and the forest of white flowers
Upon the Altar, and white lightnings of the dew...
Fallen from the petals
Seem one.

 Edith Sitwell

The bride unrumples her white dress, the minute-hand of the clock moves slowly.

Walt Whitman

This is quite possibly the most important, intricate, and beautiful dress you'll ever wear... this piece of clothing should make you feel transformed, confident, positively blissful.

Tracy Guth

The Flowers...

This is a time for flowers. May
each of them give to you not only
its beauty and fragrance, but also
the symbolic meaning that human
experience has added to them.

 Wellerman Poltarnees

I got me flowers to straw thy way;
I got me boughs off many a tree:
But thou wast up by break of day,
And brought'st thy sweets along with thee.
Can there be any day but this,
Though many sunnes to shine endeavour?
We count three hundred, but we misse:
There is but one, and that one ever.

 George Herbert

I sing of brooks, of blossoms, birds, and bowers:
Of April, May, of June, and July-flowers.
I sing of May-poles, Hock-carts, wassails, wakes,
Of bride-grooms, brides, and of their bridal cakes.

 Robert Herrick

When to Marry

Marry when the year is new,
Always loving, kind and true.
When February birds do mate,
You may wed, nor dread your fate.
If you wed when March winds blow,
Joy and sorrow both you'll know.
Marry in April when you can,
Joy for maiden and for man.
Marry in the month of May,
You will surely rue the day.
Marry when June roses blow,
Over land and sea you'll go.
They who in July do wed,
Must labour always for their bread.
Whoever wed in August be,
Many a change are sure to see.
Marry in September's shine,
Your living will be rich and fine.
If in October you do marry,
Love will come, but riches tarry.
If you wed in bleak November,
Only joy will come, remember.
When December's snows fall fast,
Marry and true love will last.

 Traditional Lines

To the June Bride

The groom is at the altar, and the organ's playing low,
Young and old, your friends are waiting, they are sitting row by row.
Now your girlhood's all behind you, in a few brief minutes more
You'll be wife to him who's waiting, through the years that lie before.

Oh, I say it not to daunt you, but to strengthen you for fate,
In the distance for your coming many heavy trials wait.
Whoso enters into marriage takes a very solemn vow
To be faithful to the other when the days are not as now.

Arm in arm you'll walk together through the lane of many years,
Side by side you'll reap life's pleasures, side by side you'll shed your tears;
'Tis a long road you'll be faring, for I've journeyed half the way,
But if love and faith sustain you, you will triumph, come what may.

There's the happy time of marriage, but to every man and wife
Also come the hurts and sorrows and the bitterness of life;
For by these your faith is tested, 'tis by these your love shall grow,
And my prayer is love shall guide you wheresoever you shall go.

Edgar A. Guest

The Wedding Day

Brightly dawns our wedding day;
Joyous hour, we give thee greeting!

 Sir William Schwenck Gilbert

Now two are becoming one,
the black night is scattered,
the eastern sky grows bright.
At last the great day has come!

 Hawaiian Song

Hear the mellow wedding bells —
Golden bells!
What a world of happiness their harmony foretells!
Through the balmy air of night
How they ring out their delight!

 Edgar Allan Poe

When the wedding march sounds the resolute approach, the
clock no longer ticks, it tolls the hour.... The figures in the aisle
are no longer individuals, they symbolize the human race.

 Anne Morrow Lindbergh

The sun-beames in the East are spred,
Leave, leave, faire Bride, your solitary bed,
No more shall you returne to it alone.

 John Donne

And you will play new songs,
plucking sweet sounds from strings;
hailing with hymns your wedding day,
you will play new songs.

 Hroswitha

A new life comes to me — bearing all glad brightness on its dawning
and giving me hope — while yet anxious thoughts of weakness and
insufficiency crowd thick into my mind.

Elizabeth Ann Jennison

A Bride's Prayer

Oh, Father, my heart is filled with a happiness so wonderful that I am
almost afraid. This is my wedding day, and I pray Thee that the beautiful
joy of this morning may never grow dim with years of regret for the step
which I am about to take. Rather, may its memories become more sweet
and tender with each passing anniversary.

 Anonymous

On Your Wedding Day

On your wedding day, you will look at yourself in the mirror, and for just a moment there will be a little girl staring back — the same freckle-faced girl who loved to jump rope and eat ice cream.

On your wedding day, you will wonder if you're ready to start this new life together. Will you make a good wife? Will he be a loving husband? So many questions flood your mind, and you begin to feel afraid.

On your wedding day, your mother will burst into your room, filled with excitement. "It's time to get ready! Hurry up, it's getting late!" Your father is still in the kitchen because he is not quite ready to say those words.

On your wedding day, your father will finally come into your room. There are tears in his eyes. He yearns for the days when he could just say, "Change into your play clothes; Dad's going to buy you a big ice-cream cone." But when he sees you in your wedding gown, it takes his breath away, and you both know it's time to go.

On your wedding day, the reception hall will be filled with friends and family. The music begins to play. Your heart is pounding so hard, and your legs are shaking. Your mom knows exactly how you feel because she felt the same on her wedding day.

Then he takes hold of your hand and your eyes lock together, and the fears of that day disappear as you become his wife.

Mary Adisano

Standing by the bridegroom's side,
With a sweet and modest pride,
See the fair and blushing bride.

In her curly hazel hair,
And on her bosom, does she wear
Snowy blossoms sweet and fair.

Oh, so wondrous pure and white,
Soft and lovely as the light
Of a summer morning bright!

                    Effie Waller Smith

The Bride...
Floating all white
beside her father
in the morning shadow of trees,
her veil flowing with laughter.

        D. H. Lawrence

She walks in beauty like the night
Of cloudless climes and starry skies;
And all that's best of dark and bright
Meets in her aspect and her eyes:
Thus mellow'd to that tender light
Which heaven to gaudy day denies.

        George Gordon, Lord Byron

# A Bride Is...

...the daughter of light...
Delightful is the sight of her,
Radiant with shining beauty.
Her garments are like spring flowers,
And a scent of sweet fragrance is diffused from them...
Truth rests upon her head.

 From The New Testament Apocrypha

...a spirit blithe as dawn; a soul astart;
A nature rich, to keep thee what thou art –
A star of beauty and a flame of power.

Robert Underwood Johnson

...the emblem of
Pure and sweet and perfect love.

Effie Waller Smith

...leaving the home of her childhood's mirth,
She hath bid farewell to her father's hearth,
Her place is now by another's side.
Bring flowers for the locks of the fair young bride!

 Felicia Dorothea Hemans

...clad in a robe of pure and spotless white...
To greet the hand to which she plights her troth,
Her soft eyes radiant with a strange delight.
The snowy veil which circles her around
Shades the sweet face from every gazer's eye,
And thus enwrapt, she passes calmly by.

Alice B. Neal

...all unveiled, save by modesty...
    in her white satin hood:
Her charms unadorned by the garland or gem,
Yet fair as the lily just plucked from its stem.

 Elizabeth Dodge Kinney

...like starlight beneath a night-cloud.

 John Rollin Ridge

...beautiful with joy, and warm with tenderness.

 William Brian Hooker

♡ The Wedding ♡

A moment of calm
smoothes my heart
as I hear the harmony
in the music that signals
my entrance.
I feel as though I am
embarking on a journey
that I have envisioned
all my life.
I see you standing in front of me.
You grasp my hand,
and we begin to speak
utterances of our love
and commitment.
It is at this moment and
because of the silent knowledge
in our eyes
that I know we are here
purely for each other.
Though we stand before
a crowd of familiar faces,
our souls privately celebrate
as we complete the bond
that has been forming for so long
by binding our two lives together
with a promise of friendship
    and devotion.

 Andrea Dayton

If I had to live my entire life in just one day
I would choose today
If I had one dream to fulfill
it would be this dream
If I could be with only one person
it would be you

I would speak
so only you would hear
I would laugh
so only you would laugh in return
I would cry
so only you would hug away the hurt

If all my wishes were to come true
they have this moment
If luck ever shined in my life
it is now
If sorrow comes tomorrow
I have already loved a lifetime... today.

 Kelly Allyson Schwenk

*I take you to be
my wedded husband...*

Summer's warm breeze
    Is beckoning a new life
Now our thoughts will rendezvous
    Into a beautiful dream
As you take my hand
    A soft strength overwhelms me
To know that I'm loved
    For this day we pledge
Ourselves in love... forever.

 Lanny Allen

Come stand by my side
where I'm going
Take my hand
if I stumble and fall
It's the strength that you share
when you're growing
that gives me what I need
most of all.

Hoyt Axton

My Heart's Song

My darling take my heart
Where we'll never be apart;
Hold it within your breast
Where passions of life cannot molest.
I'll cherish all your many charms;
Embraced within your loving arms
So keep my love safe and strong
And listen to my heart's song,
My darling, please take my heart.

Gracia Lowell Bauer

To have and to hold from this day forward...

Oh, the comfort, the inexpressible comfort of feeling safe with a person; having neither to weigh thoughts nor measure words, but to pour them all out, just as they are, chaff and grain together, knowing that a faithful hand will take and sift them, keep what is worth keeping, and then, with the breath of kindness, blow the rest away.

George Eliot

I give you my hand!
I give you my love more precious than money;
I give you myself before preaching or law.
Will you give me yourself? Will you come travel with me?
Shall we stick by each other as long as we live?

Walt Whitman

Now join your hands, and with your hands your hearts.

William Shakespeare

For better, for worse...

Marriage... hath in it less of beauty but more of safety than the single life; it hath more care, but less danger; it is more merry and more sad, is fuller of sorrows and fuller of joys; it lies under more burdens, but is supported by all the strengths of love and charity, and those burdens are delightful.

 Jeremy Taylor

What power has love but forgiveness?
In other words
by its intervention
what has been done
can be undone.
What good is it otherwise?

 William Carlos Williams

The quarrels of lovers are the renewal of love.

 Terence

I took the good times, I'll take the bad times
I'll take you just the way you are.

Billy Joel

For richer, for poorer...

Gifts alone
do not entice love;
parting does not discourage love;
poverty does not chase love.

 Kahlil Gibran

In marriage do thou be wise: prefer the person before
money, virtue before beauty, the mind before the body; then
thou hast a wife, a friend, a companion, a second self.

 William Penn

It is a good thing to be
rich and to be strong,
but it is a better thing
to be loved.

 Euripides

In sickness, and in health...

What greater thing is there for two human souls than to feel that they are joined for life – to strengthen each other in all labor, to rest on each other in all sorrow, to minister to each other in all pain, to be one with each other in silent, unspeakable memories at the moment of the last parting.

George Eliot

Two are better than one, because they have a good reward for their toil. For if they fall, one will lift up the other.

Ecclesiastes 4:9-10 (NRSV)

There may come times when one partner is heartbroken or ailing, and the love of the other may resemble the tender caring of a parent for a child.

Edmund O'Neill

We seek the comfort of another. Someone to share and share the life we choose. Someone to help us through the never-ending attempt to understand ourselves. And in the end, someone to comfort us along the way.

Marlin Finch Lupus

To love and to cherish, till death do us part...

To love someone deeply
Gives you strength.

Being loved by someone deeply
Gives you courage.

Lao-Tzu

Love and harmony combine,
And around our souls intwine,
While thy branches mix with mine,
And our roots together join.

Joys upon our branches sit,
Chirping loud, and singing sweet;
Like gentle streams beneath our feet
Innocence and virtue meet.

William Blake

Let me not to the marriage of true minds
Admit impediments. Love is not love
Which alters when it alteration finds,
Or bends with the remover to remove:
O, no! it is an ever-fixed mark,
That looks on tempests and is never shaken;
It is the star to every wandering bark,
Whose worth's unknown, although his height be taken.
Love's not Time's fool, though rosy lips and cheeks
Within his bending sickle's compass come;
Love alters not with his brief hours and weeks,
But bears it out even to the edge of doom.
If this is error, and upon me prov'd,
I never write, nor no man ever lov'd.

William Shakespeare

Promises of Love

Love is patient, love is kind.
It does not envy, it does not boast,
it is not proud. It is not rude, it is not
self-seeking, it is not easily angered,
it keeps no record of wrongs. Love
does not delight in evil but rejoices
with the truth. It always protects,
always trusts, always hopes,
always perseveres.

Love never fails.

 1 Corinthians 13:4-8 (NIV)

I offer this: you've given me
A chance to contemplate that Sea
Of Faith; bless God for having now
With no fear of an ebb below.

I promise this: a legacy.
That all tomorrows granted me
Shall ripen richer deeper care
Because this moment you were here.

 Henry J. Amgwert

Doubt thou the stars are fire,
Doubt that the sun doth move;
Doubt truth to be a liar,
But never doubt I love.

 William Shakespeare

You are my husband
My feet shall run because of you.
My feet, dance because of you.
My heart shall beat because of you.
My eyes, see because of you.
My mind, think because of you.
And I shall love because of you.

 — Eskimo Love Song

Now you will feel no rain
For each of you will be
    shelter to the other.
Now you will feel no cold
For each of you will be
    warmth to the other.
Now you will feel no loneliness
For each of you will be
    companionship to the other.
Now you are two persons
But there is only one life between you.

Go now to your dwelling place
To enter into the days of your life together.

 American Indian Wedding Prayer

You have become mine forever. Yes, we have
become partners. I have become yours. Hereafter,
I cannot live without you. Do not live without me.
Let us share the joys. We are word and meaning,
united. You are thought and I am sound.

May the nights be honey-sweet for us; may
the mornings be honey-sweet for us; may the
earth be honey-sweet for us; may the heavens
be honey-sweet for us.

May the plants be honey-sweet for us; may the
sun be all honey for us; may the cows yield us
honey-sweet milk!

As the heavens are stable, as the earth is stable,
as the mountains are stable, as the whole universe
is stable, so may our union be permanently settled.

 From the Hindu Marriage Ritual of "Seven Steps"

A Wedding Song…
Give Yourself to Love

Kind friends all gathered 'round
    there's something I would say
That what brings us together here
    has blessed us all today
Love has made a circle
    that holds us all inside
Where strangers are as family
    and loneliness can't hide

You must give yourself to love
    if love is what you're after
Open up your heart
    to the tears and laughter
    and give yourself to love
Give yourself to love

I've walked these mountains in the rain
    I've learned to love the wind
I've been up before the sunrise
    to watch the day begin
I always knew I'd find you
    though I never did know how
But like sunshine on a cloudy day
    you stand before me now

So give yourself to love
    if love is what you're after
Open up your heart
    to the tears and laughter
    and give yourself to love
Give yourself to love

Love is born in fire
    it's planted like a seed
Love can't give you everything
    but it gives you what you need
Love comes when you are ready
    love comes when you're afraid
It will be your greatest teacher
    the best friend you have made

So give yourself to love
    if love is what you're after
Open up your heart
    to the tears and laughter
    and give yourself to love
Give yourself to love.

 Kate Wolf

After the Wedding

Understand, I'll slip quietly
away from the noisy crowd
when I see the pale
stars rising, blooming, over the oaks.

I'll pursue solitary pathways
through the pale twilit meadows,
with only this one dream:
You come too.

 — Rainer Maria Rilke

Tonight is a night of union and also of scattering of the stars,
for a bride is coming from the sky: the full moon.
The sky is an astrolabe, and the Law is Love.

 Jalal Al-Din Rumi

Nay, but she sleeps like a bride, and dreams her dreams
Of perfect things.

 — D. H. Lawrence

Today I married my best friend,
Our bond complete, it hath no end,
We share one soul, we share one heart,
A perfect time — a perfect start.

With these rings we share together,
Love so close to last forever,
This special day — two special hearts,
Let nothing keep this love apart.

 — Rachel Elizabeth Cooper

Special times and special places, special friends together;
the moments pass so quickly, but the memories last forever.

— Anonymous

The ring is on my hand,
And the wreath is on my brow;
Satins and jewels grand
Are all at my command,
And I am happy now.

 Edgar Allan Poe

From this day forward,
You shall not walk alone.
My heart will be your shelter,
And my arms will be your home.

 Anonymous

In the Heart of a Bride

I only knew I loved and was loved, only that we wanted to be with one another, touch one another, steal hours to be together, talk or not talk it did not matter.

 Rumer Godden

I have won the love of one of the best men I ever met. Oh! Life seems so bright and happy to me now, and the future seems much brighter.

Katie Reed McWilliams

He is the only person of whom I think with consistent tenderness. I can say with truth that I have never, never cherished a harsh thought about him.... He has complete power over my heart, though not over my spirit. It is real tenderness I feel for him.

 Vita Sackville-West

He's more myself than I am. Whatever our souls are made of, his and mine are the same.... If all else perished and *he* remained, I should still continue to be, and if all else remained, and he were annihilated, the universe would turn to a might stranger.... He's always, always in my mind; not as a pleasure to myself, but as my own being.

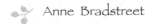 Emily Brontë

If ever two were one, then surely we;
If ever man were loved by wife, then thee;
If ever wife was happy in a man,
Compare with me, ye women, if you can.
I prize thy love more than whole mines of gold,
Or all the riches that the East doth hold.
My love is such that rivers cannot quench,
Nor aught but love from thee give recompense.
Thy love is such I can no way repay;
The heavens reward thee manifold, I pray.
Then while we live in love let's so persevere
That when we live no more we may live ever.

Anne Bradstreet

In the Heart of a Groom

My whole being is permeated, is renewed, is leavened with this love and with every breath I draw its noble influence makes of me a better man.

Mark Twain

I dreamed of a wedding of elaborate elegance; a church filled with flowers and friends. I asked him what kind of wedding he wished for; he said one that would make me his wife.

Anonymous

My romance doesn't have to have
A moon in the sky
My romance doesn't need
A blue lagoon standing by
No month of May, no twinkling stars
No hideaway, no soft guitars

My romance doesn't need
A castle rising in Spain
Nor a dance to a constantly
Surprising refrain
Wide awake I can make
My most fantastic dreams come true

My romance doesn't need a thing but you

Lorenz Hart

Really I began the day
Not with a man's wish: "May this day be different";
But with the bird's wish: "May this day
Be the same day, the day of my life."

 Randall Jarrell

You shall go with me, newly-married bride,
And gaze upon a merrier multitude....
Where beauty has no ebb, decay no flood,
But joy is wisdom, time an endless song.

William Butler Yeats

To my bride, I give you my heart
Sharing love each day, from the very start
To my bride, I give you my kiss
Filling each day with joy and bliss
To my bride, I give you my being
To love, to play, to work and to sing
To my bride, I give you my mind
Learning each day to be more kind
To my bride, I give you my soul
Growing together to be more whole
To my bride, I give you my life
Rejoicing each day that you are my wife.

Steven Reiser

The Challenges of Marriage

To live in love is life's greatest challenge. It.... will require that you continually have the subtlety of the very wise, the flexibility of the child, the sensitivity of the artist, the understanding of the philosopher, the acceptance of the saint, the tolerance of the dedicated, the knowledge of the scholar, and the fortitude of the certain.

Leo Buscaglia

Understanding the true meaning of marriage
Is not looking through rose-colored glasses.
It's going in with your eyes wide open
And both feet planted firmly on the ground.

Karen Pettenuzzo

Fear less, hope more;
Whine less, breathe more;
Talk less, say more;
Hate less, love more;
And all good things are yours.

Swedish Proverb

I would like to have engraved inside every wedding band *Be kind to one another*. This is the Golden Rule of marriage and the secret of making love last through the years.

Randolph Ray

Seek not to create for each other a new mold that can only fit with much discomfort and pain. Accept the other as they are, as you would have yourself accepted.

 Ginny and Manny Feldman

Let there be spaces in your togetherness,
And let the winds of heaven dance between you.

Love one another, but make not a bond of love:
Let it rather be a moving sea between the shores of
    your souls.
Fill each other's cup but drink not from one cup.
Give one another of your bread but eat not from the
    same loaf.
Sing and dance together and be joyous, but let each
    one of you be alone,
Even as the strings of a lute are alone though they
    quiver with the same music.

Give your hearts, but not into each other's keeping.
For only the hand of life can contain your hearts.
And stand together yet not too near together:
For the pillars of the temple stand apart,
And the oak tree and the cypress grow not in each
    other's shadow.

Kahlil Gibran

Grow old along with me, the best is yet to be.

Robert Browning

The sum which two married people owe to one another defies calculation. It is an infinite debt, which can only be discharged through all eternity.

Johann Wolfgang von Goethe

Love seems the swiftest, but it is the slowest of all growths. No man or woman really knows what perfect love is until they have been married a quarter of a century.

Mark Twain

When you and I were wed on that fair day
We stood alone upon a whirling star,
Taut heartstrings thrumming like a wild guitar,
Young wonder veiling all the starry way,
There, lost in unforgettable embrace,
We quenched a thirst of lonely desert years,
A golden circlet, diamonded with tears,
Became another life-link for the race.

Ann Woodbury Hafen

To keep one sacred flame
    Through life unchilled, unmoved,
To love in wintry age, the same
    As first in youth we loved,
To feel that we adore
    Even to fond excess,
That though the heart would break
        with more,
    It could not live with less.

Thomas Moore

In Marriage

Cherish each other
in big ways and in small ways,
and never forget the magic
of those three little words: "I love you."
In marriage, remember that
it is the little things that make the difference...
Don't forget the birthdays and the anniversaries.
An occasional note means a lot.
Share each other's life — even the small details —
for too often we forget
that day-after-day becomes
year-after-year, and then it's gone.
Give each other room to grow...
We all need our time alone.
Keep strong your faith in each other;
time has a funny way of testing us,
and it's faith that gets us through.
Respect one another...
This world could always use more of that.
Speak your mind honestly, openly,
but with kindness,
for angry words are scars that may never heal.
Trust each other;
let your trust be your rock.
Most of all, each day...
be sure to hold each other
and fall in love all over again.

 Julia Escobar

ACKNOWLEDGMENTS

We gratefully acknowledge the permission granted by the following authors, publishers, and authors' representatives to reprint poems or excerpts from their publications.

The Mark Twain Foundation for "A marriage...," "My whole being...," and "Love seems the swiftest..." from THE LOVE LETTERS OF MARK TWAIN, edited by Dixon Wector. Copyright © 1947, 1949 by The Mark Twain Foundation. All rights reserved.

HarperCollins Publishers, Inc., for "The whole process..." from FROM THIS DAY FORWARD by Cokie and Steve Roberts. Copyright © 2000 by Cokie and Steve Roberts. And for "I only knew..." from A TIME TO DANCE, NO TIME TO WEEP by Rumer Godden. Copyright © 1987 by Rumer Godden. All rights reserved.

The UltimateWedding.com community for "We made a decision...." Copyright © 1996-2000 by UltimatePublishing.com. All rights reserved.

Judy Edwards for "Sitting on my bed..." and "I am who I am...." Copyright © 2000 by Judy Edwards. All rights reserved.

Farrar, Straus and Giroux, LLC, for "Are there any brothers..." from "Wedding Day" from EARTHLY PARADISE by Colette, edited by Robert Phelps. Translation copyright © 1966, renewed 1994 by Farrar, Straus and Giroux, Inc. And for "Really I began..." from "A Man Meets A Woman in the Street" from THE COMPLETE POEMS by Randall Jarrell. Copyright © 1969, renewed 1997 by Mary von S. Jarrell.

Kym A. Innes for "For My Daughter, on Your Wedding Day." Copyright © 2000 by Kym A. Innes. All rights reserved.

Michael Friedman Publishing Group, Inc., for "This is quite possibly..." from FOR YOUR WEDDING: DRESSES by Tracy Guth. Copyright © 2000 by Tracy Guth. All rights reserved.

Stewart, Tabori, and Chang for "This is a time..." by Wellerman Poltarnees from BOUQUETS: A YEAR OF FLOWERS FOR THE BRIDE by Marsha Heckman. Copyright © 2000 by Marsha Heckman. All rights reserved.

Regnery Publishing, Inc., for "To the June Bride" from COLLECTED VERSE OF EDGAR A. GUEST. Copyright © 1934 by Regnery Publishing. All rights reserved.

Harcourt, Inc., for "When the wedding..." from DEARLY BELOVED: A THEME AND VARIATIONS by Anne Morrow Lindbergh. Copyright © 1962 by Harcourt, Inc., renewed 1990 by Anne Morrow Lindbergh. All rights reserved.

Mary Adisano for "On Your Wedding Day." Copyright © 2000 by Mary Adisano. All rights reserved.

Oxford University Press, source for "Standing by..." and "...the emblem of..." from COLLECTED WORKS OF EFFIE WALLER SMITH. Copyright © 1991 by Oxford University Press. All rights reserved.

Westminster John Knox Press and The Lutterworth Press for "...the daughter of light..." from THE NEW TESTAMENT APOCRYPHA, edited by Wilhelm Schneemelcher and Edgar Hennecke. Copyright © 1990 by Westminster John Knox Press.

Roth Publishing, Inc., and Poem Finder® (www.PoemFinder.com) for "...beautiful with joy..." by William Brian Hooker. Copyright © 2000 by Roth Publishing, Inc. All rights reserved.

Irving Music for "Come stand..." from "Less Than The Song" by Hoyt Axton. Copyright © 1972 by Lady Jane Music. All rights reserved.

New Directions Publishing Corp. and Carcanet Press Ltd. for "What power has love..." by William Carlos Williams from COLLECTED POEMS 1939-1962, VOLUME II. Copyright © 1944 by William Carlos Williams. All rights reserved.

Impulsive Music for "I took the good times..." from "Just the Way You Are" by Billy Joel. Copyright © 1977 by Impulsive Music. All rights reserved.

Citadel Press, an imprint of Kensington Publishing Corp. for "Gifts alone..." from A TREASURY OF KAHLIL GIBRAN. Copyright © 1951, 1979 by Citadel Press. All rights reserved.

Another Sundown Publishing Company for "Give Yourself to Love" by Kate Wolf. Copyright © 1982 by Another Sundown Publishing Company. All rights reserved.

Random House, Inc., for "Understand, I'll slip quietly..." from LETTERS TO A YOUNG POET by Rainer Maria Rilke. Copyright © 1984 by Stephen Mitchell. All rights reserved.

The University of Chicago Press for "Tonight is a night..." by Jalal Al-Din Rumi from MYSTICAL POEMS OF RUMI, translated by A. J. Arberry. Copyright © 1968 by A. J. Arberry. All rights reserved.

Scribner, a division of Simon & Schuster, for "He is the only..." by Vita Sackville-West from PORTRAIT OF A MARRIAGE by Nigel Nicolson. Copyright © 1974 by Nigel Nicolson. All rights reserved.

Williamson Music for "My romance..." from "My Romance" by Richard Rodgers and Lorenz Hart. Copyright © 1935 by Williamson Music and Lorenz Hart Music (administered by Williamson Music). Copyright renewed. All rights reserved.

Steven Reiser for "To my bride...." Copyright © 2000 by Steven Reiser. All rights reserved.

The Leo F. Buscaglia Foundation for "To live in love..." from LOVE by Leo F. Buscaglia. Copyright © 1972 by Leo F. Buscaglia, Inc. All rights reserved.

Simon & Schuster for "I would like to have..." from MY LITTLE CHURCH AROUND THE CORNER by Dr. Randolph J. H. Ray in collaboration with Villa Stiles. Copyright © 1957 by Randolph J. H. Ray. All rights reserved.

Ginny and Manny Feldman for "Seek not to..." from "The Marriage Creed." Copyright © 1971 by Emanuel M. Feldman, licensed MFCC/MFT, and Virginia L. Feldman. All rights reserved.

Alfred A. Knopf, a division of Random House, Inc., and the Gibran National Committee, Beirut, Lebanon, for "Let there be spaces..." from THE PROPHET by Kahlil Gibran. Copyright © 1923 by Kahlil Gibran and renewed 1951 by Administrators C.T.A. of Kahlil Gibran Estate, and Mary G. Gibran. All rights reserved.

A careful effort has been made to trace the ownership of selections used in this anthology in order to obtain permission to reprint copyrighted materials and give proper credit to the copyright owners. If any error or omission has occurred, it is completely inadvertent, and we would like to make corrections in future editions provided that written notification is made to the publisher:

SPS STUDIOS, INC., P.O. Box 4549, Boulder, Colorado 80306.